Think, Follow and Grow

by: Dora Gomory

Copyright © 2012 Dora Gomory

All rights reserved.

ISBN-10: 1986007839
ISBN-13: 978-1986007832

Hard work is success.

Success is freedom.

Freedom is happiness.

Never give up your dreams!

CONTENTS

1	Why is this book for you?	1
2	The wish	4
3	From London to city of Poole	10
4	The inspiration	14
5	Never give up	20
6	Way to success	28
7	The motivation for everyone	38

WHY IS THIS BOOK FOR YOU?

It took a long time for me to decide to write this book. And let me tell you, it wasn't easy for me. I always wanted to share my happiness, my success and it was always in my head as I wanted to help others with my story – my story of success, my dream. I've never been a chatterbox, and I will not exaggerate. I can promise that I will try my best to tell you how I started and what I become. I will tell you everything in detail so that you can see and appreciate the transformation in my life.

Some people dream about making billions. They think they can be rich if they are either born rich or they are extraordinarily talented. Some people feel that only lucky ones become rich, but this is not true. Actually, most of the people today are looking for shortcuts – shortcuts for everything. They want shortcuts to earn money, shortcuts becoming famous. But as the popular saying goes, "Rome wasn't built in a day". Everything takes time, and to keep patience is the key.

I can certainly understand these conceptions, although I strongly believe that there are many more ways to become rich. But I would like to hold on here for a minute before I move forward with my story. I want to tell you something important – something that will help you follow your dreams. I think being rich is quite a relative thing. You can be tagged as "rich" if you have wealth; you can be tagged as "rich" if you are happy and contented in life. While most of the people think, richness comes with money, I feel richness comes with happiness. If you ask me, I would say I am happy when I am my own boss. I am happy when I have plenty of time for my personal life. I am happy when I earn by doing something that makes me happy, and not something that I force myself to do. So, this is what "being rich" means to me. And its time you too decide it for yourself. Think what it is that makes you happy and work towards it. Make it your goal and try to achieve it – no matter what it takes. So, take a lead and define this word "rich". Decide when and what you would like to do.

Okay, let's go ahead with this book. But if you feel it's not something you would like to read, you can stop here and never read this book any further. If you have decided to go ahead, thank you. If this book is what you need, I am ready to share with you my story of how I actually started building up my little crochet world and succeeded. I do not want to brag about myself, but I will share with you my true story. I will tell you about all those days when I was really lost, and then those days when I felt great. I feel it's all the matter of time. After every night, there comes a morning- a day when all the darkness fades away and brings along with it light – light and hope. If you stay put during that dark night, you will come out shining during the bright day. So, have faith in you.

THE WISH

I was no different from you or anyone else. I was just an ordinary person, seeking to earn a living and better the existing quality of my life. And this is a dream of almost every other person in this world. So, I wasn't expecting too much from my life.

Like a vast majority of the people in the world, I too was born under ordinary circumstances. I led a fairly normal life like most of my peers and acquaintances too. But I had the ambition to make something more of myself. I have no problems with a conventional life but I felt, and still believe, that if life has more to offer you and you have the thirst for it, then with ingenuity and some hard work, you ought to get that more rather than grumpily settling for the ordinary.

Even today, I do not regard myself as someone extraordinarily brilliant or much better than average! I feel I am just another person, as each of us has dreams, and even I had one. So, I haven't changed from what I used to be. If at all anything has changed, it is my attitude towards living my life. And that's because of the choices I made, after trying out various things.

I didn't know what I wanted to be. Frankly, I just did not know! All I wanted was financial freedom. I wanted to be self-dependent and live my life my way. I didn't want to depend on someone for everything; I didn't want others to help me in fulfilling my dreams. And in quest of this financial freedom, I kept toying with various ideas, such as becoming a businessperson and earning loads of money, becoming an author, writing best-selling novels and self-publishing, etc., but could never reach any concrete conclusion and an effective plan. Nevertheless, I was completely sure of one thing, and that was, that I wished to travel the world. Oh, yes, travelling across the world was my hobby and I had a bucket list of places that I wanted to explore! And I wanted a lot of money to do that. I wanted financial freedom to travel the world. However, the place that topped this list was the UK. I do not know why this place fascinated me so much, for I had never seen it before, except in pictures. Nonetheless, I wished to go there. I had decided that as soon as I had enough money in my pockets, I would zip off to this distant place! In fact, I really wanted to even settle down there, prior to travelling to other places for short tours.

Of course, my family tried to dissuade me from indulging in this foolish (in their opinion) dream, suggesting that there was no place better than home. And that whatever I want to do there, can be done by staying in hometown also. Additionally, I was a 'girl'. I would just lose myself in the huge, bad world outside the home! It was not safe for me to venture into unknown places. I would find sufficient opportunities for personal and professional growth in nearby cities. There was no need for me to move so far away.

In those days, there were several times I felt quite different from the people I lived with. Having said that, my eagerness to make more out myself, get more out of life did not alter the love and respect I had for anybody. I knew that whatever my parents and family members had to say to me came from a loving place in their heart. What malice, or what connivance could they have?! There were, of course, a few people who didn't want me to make the changes in my life simply because they were jealous of me, or because they had wanted to do it themselves but weren't able to. I know now for a fact that for every 10 people who want the best out of life for you, there may be 1 or 2 who don't. I didn't bother to let their views or words affect me in any manner. What my family said and did is all that mattered. And this mantra holds good even today! Out of concern and love for me, my family tried convincing me in different ways that I had everything I could get out of life; I shouldn't dream of flying off to distant lands when I already had everything that a girl could ask for.

However, all those reasons could never convince me to stay back. I wanted to fly; I wanted to be unique and different from everybody else. I wanted to explore this world on my own. And luckily, I did get the opportunity to launch my dream. Soon after completing my schooling at the local school, I did my masters from one of the universities. I wanted to complete my studies, and that topped my To-Do list for time being. I always wanted to be financially independent and hence, I started looking out for a temporary job till I come up with some great. I was offered to teach in one of the schools, and I accepted this opportunity with open hands. I then started working as a teacher, right after completing my studies, for a year. But as I mentioned, this was just a temporary solution to earn a living. I wanted something more from life.

I wasn't contented with what I was doing and my ultimate plan was to move out and travel the world. When I got some bucks in my hand, I started working on my plan. I researched about various places but somehow my heart was stuck at one spot on the map. Could you guess what it was? Yes, it was the United Kingdom – my dream place.

So, I decided to move to another city and London was my destination. Of course, it wasn't that easy but I had managed to persuade my family to let me go! My arguments included stuff like, "Girls were proving to be better than boys in many fields in this contemporary world, everybody deserved equal opportunities to progress, I wanted to travel and see the world", etc. But I somehow managed to convince them and started on my journey from there.

Exhilaration! Nervousness! Giddiness! Happiness! I was bombarded with these feelings and much more. Finding an opportunity that worked in the larger scheme of things that I had dreamt of was a true godsend. I worked sincerely and hard for it, but still, such surprises knock off your feet for a while, don't they?! I was hit by varying emotions, sometimes alternatively, sometimes together. I was a mix of emotions, but my goal and ambition remained clearly in sight. The edges around that picture never blurred even for a minute!

After a hiatus at home, I was glad to be able to go ahead with my dream plan with the blessing and support of my family. They had known my dream for so many years now, but they had only realised how genuinely passionate I was about it very recently, I supposed. With a mind relieved at the family end, I took to spreading my wings in the United Kingdom. To this day, I don't know why this country is so magical to me, but I don't think I will tire of this place! Of course, I am still passionate about seeing the rest of the world because there are marvellous things to be found in so many other places. But this country would also have a special place in my heart and imagination!

I knew that it is not easy to just go to another country and find a job. I knew I had to struggle for my survival there. But I was very much okay with it. I wanted to do it; I wanted to at least give myself a chance. All these thoughts kept running through my mind throughout the journey and finally, I landed in London. Yes, I landed in London. For once, I couldn't believe I was in a place I had always dreamt of. But it was time to get back to reality. I was in London, but now what? What should be the next step? Where should I go? What should I do?

First things first, I started looking for a cheap place to stay in, as well as arrange for regular meals. I didn't mind staying anywhere as I didn't want to waste money on accommodation – it wasn't important. The most important task was to look for a decent job; look for options for gainful employment. I also hoped that I would be able to make new friends quickly, for I was bound to feel alone in an alien country, wherein I knew no one. My family prayed for my safety, success and happiness, and I prayed for myself too!

FROM LONDON TO CITY OF POOLE

When I first stepped into fast-paced, noisy and busy London, I was completely bewildered and rather terrified! I had never been able to comprehend why people felt the need to hurry here, hurry there, and hurry everywhere! I felt as if everyone is just running all the time. Running for? Running behind? I didn't know and I could never understand. But yes, the life was pretty hectic and fast moving.

Furthermore, I realised that my ears were rather sensitive to noise, and this was probably because I had stayed in the peaceful countryside all my life so far. Don't get me wrong. The pictures of cobblestones pavements on rainy days with a tall, glass-enclosed lamppost, the soft, the bite in the wind and the gorgeous, open view harbours – these fascinated me as I reached this country that is so different from my own. Just when I had seen all the marvels there were to see in this beautiful, bustling city, out popped another one!

You know how you constantly keep turning your head here and there because you are just surrounded by new things and people? I'd turned into a bit of a staring pigeon myself! The people spoke and walked differently, their clothes made me want to haunt every single sale that I could afford (and even those I couldn't sometimes!), and their food items were truly eye-openers for me because I'd never been introduced to such a different food culture! Oh! I could go on and on about the new things that enthralled me and made me love every bit of this charming foreign land that I'd transported myself too!

However, I had a career to build, a foreign land to make it in; I had made my choice and had to stick to it. I will not bug you with details about how I went through customs or wandered helplessly for days to make this happen. I started looking out for an affordable place to stay in, and suitable employment. And well, I did manage to find a place for myself with the help of someone I had met during my journey from my home country. Another person helped me find employment for earning a living. I could not crib about the kinds of jobs I was handling, big or small, for I needed money to keep my stomach well fed, pay the rent, and so on. Additionally, I would have to sideline local or international sightseeing tours for the time being! What was important was to attain financial freedom!

***

This scenario continued for at least a year or so. The hustle and bustle of the big city no longer bothered my nerves, and I was quite comfortable. Yes, stress did make uninvited entries into my life occasionally. I even suffered from insomnia or sleeplessness at times. Nonetheless, I accepted everything as 'part of life'. Then, something wonderful happened! I had developed a reasonably big social circle by now. Through this circle, I came to know about an employment opportunity far away from London. It was in a place called Poole in Dorset. For some time, I debated with myself about staying in London or moving away from it. I could be giving up a reasonably comfortable life for an unknown one in an unknown place, thereby ushering in deep regret. I consulted with several people, and then took a final decision. I was ready to move to Poole. After all, I had left my native place to seek a better future in a land that I had never seen. So, what was stopping me from taking this decision now? I just needed the same courage now!

I packed my bags and moved to the city of Poole. Poole, to my astonishment, turned out to be gloriously peaceful, beautiful, relaxed and calm city. In fact, it had been ridiculous of me to harbour such doubts about this quiet town in the countryside! It reminded me of home so much, that I even became homesick for some time! Yes, I was missing my home probably for the first time after landing in this country.

I got a place to stay in Poole and eventually, I started liking it. I became less stressful and even began to sleep much better. Although the wages were not as healthy as they should have been, I managed to eke out a living. The fact that the place was far less expensive than London helped me save some bucks. In short, I was happy! But I didn't forget about my dreams. I did not stop keeping a keen lookout for opportunities to earn more. After all, it was necessary to keep one's finances in order in this fast-changing and fast-paced world, as well as learn new skills whenever one gained a chance to do so. So, I had my eyes and ears open – always!

THE INSPIRATION

Something happened quite suddenly and unexpectedly one day, while I was out for grocery shopping for the week. It happened this way. I was engaged in purchasing groceries, as was my do every week. This particular week, I decided to pay a visit to the nearby newspaper stand too. Now, I was definitely not the kind of person to peruse newspapers every day or browse through different magazines week after week. Call it instinct, or call it the premonition, but I just could not prevent myself from going to the newspaper stand that day! I wanted to look around and see what I could find.

While wandering in between the rows at the stand, my eyes espied a craft magazine nestling amongst the newspapers. I went nearer and pulled it out. I discovered that it was a small package, containing a magazine on crochet and knitting, a single knitting needle, a crochet hook and six balls of yarn. I stood there for quite a while, just staring at the package in my hand. It brought back good memories of childhood. I had learnt knitting at school. My teachers had seen to it. I felt that I would have no difficulty in handling the balls of yarn that accompanied the knitting and crochet magazine. However, my mind was unable to decide what to do at that particular time. Therefore, I replaced the magazine and the accompanying accessories in the newspaper rack and returned to the grocery shop to buy what I wanted. Soon enough, I forgot about the entire incident. Even today, some people knowingly nod their heads and tell me it's "destiny" that took me to the newspaper stand that day and seek out something that I'd never generally do. Destiny or not, all I know I'm glad I went off the beaten track that day! You'll see where it led me to in a bit.

The weeks just passed by, and my life continued as usual. It was a humdrum life, wherein I used to wake up in the morning, complete my chores, go to work, return home, eat and sleep. Between spending time at work and spending time at work, I also managed to get some cooking done and do the laundry. God, the day-to-day routine was getting boring and dull! Ah, really so dull that I really wanted to do something. However, for the moment, at least, I could not think of any drastic change in employment or residence. I had to abide my time, before putting any new plan into action. However, sometimes (once in every 2 months), to get rid of all the boredom, I used to spice up with a nice day out with my boyfriend.

Then one day, without warning, I fell really sick. It was wintertime, and the weather was playing havoc with everyone's health! The terrible cold managed to penetrate my respiratory system, leaving me with a severe chest infection. The outcome was predictable. I was bed-ridden for weeks. Apart from the fact that I regretted not having profitable employment, I was sure to die of sheer boredom too! I kept wondering how long I would be able to read books or watch television, without going insane! From the very second day of my illness, I decided that the situation was quite hopeless, and I could do nothing about it.

When my boyfriend asked me, what he could do to cheer me up, I suddenly recalled the magazine and its accompaniments that I had seen at the newspaper stand on that day. I requested him to somehow get the package for me. Happy to be of service to me, he obliged. An hour later, the magazine, the needle, hook and balls of yarn were in my hands.

I opened the magazine eagerly, highly motivated to begin my first knitting project ever since I had left the skill behind in elementary school. However, there was a major problem. Yes, you guessed it right! For the life of me, I simply could not remember what my elementary school teacher had taught me! It all seemed so long ago. I specifically found casting off the stitches to be terribly difficult. I read the instructions given in the magazine, repeatedly. After every reading, I began my practice once again. Nonetheless, it was all perfectly hopeless! I could not get my fingers to obey the detailed instructions at all. What was I to do? Could reading other instruction booklets help me? Maybe, they could! Therefore, I began to browse through various books on knitting, hoping to recall all that I had learnt at school. Unfortunately, nothing worked at all!

Think, Follow and Grow

Then a sudden inspiration struck me! If books and magazines could not help me, maybe watching videos would. Therefore, I got hold of some videos, which demonstrated knitting patterns in elaborate detail. And thanks to all the people and the power of these social media platforms that I could get some help. After watching a few of them, I felt encouraged to begin my knitting ventures all over again. I felt confident that I would be able to handle all the diverse aspects of knitting, including casting off stitches. If someone were to ask me how my success story was woven, I wouldn't attribute it all to the crochet stitches and knots that I've become accustomed to now. I'd say it had a lot to do with my perennially inquisitive mind.

The videos that I looked at were really helpful. They help me constructively make use of my time refreshing memories of a skill that I was fond of and had lost touch with.

Towards this end, therefore, I began knitting a snowman. There was no particular reason for choosing this pattern. I just thought I would go for it. Amazingly, I completed it too! True, if you were to see it, you would comment that you had never seen such an ugly-looking snowman in your life, but I was happy! I was proud of the fact that I had not given up and brought the project to successful completion. It sufficed to motivate me to become a big knitter in future. I promised myself that people, like you, would be able to easily recognise what I intended to display through my varied knitting yarns and patterns.

My success with knitting emboldened me. Funny, now that

I think back to that day, how much of a hero figure that snowman symbolised. I'd lit a fire within me to experiment with something new, something fascinating, and an art form that is highly customisable. Crochet can be used to make pretty tea coasters and jewellery, but it can also be used to make the lace-like fringe for a dress worth thousands of pounds. Now, I desired to become skilled at crochet too. The magazine had detailed advice to offer in this arena too. Therefore, I should find everything easy to handle. At the same time, despite my euphoria at discovering hidden talents, I had to be honest with myself. I had never touched a crochet hook in my life. Obviously, then, I would not be able to manage it skilfully, considering, that, a crochet hook was smaller and more delicate than the knitting needle in appearance. Nonetheless, I would not give up without trying! I went back to reading books and watching videos, focussing on crochet for a beginner this time.

I spent hours poring over the books and videos during my spare time. I had even taken to making tiny little notes that I'd stick to the nearest handy surface in my house, or put them neatly down in a book. I wasn't just learning how to make my fingers more nimble to achieve the complex crocheting standards, but I was also analysing the other techniques I could use to make my work better. For example, some of the videos and books talked about selecting the right hook to get the right stitches. Selecting the right wool or material to crochet, the colour combinations that would be most appealing, how the crochet creations can be accessorised to complete their look or seem more interesting – there is so much more than what meets the eye. And I was determined to learn them all and be good at this craft I had fallen in love with.

It may seem rather hard to believe, but after the first few lessons, I became hooked to the crochet hook! It was as if my life began and ended with crochet! I literally breathed, ate and slept crochet! Every morning, I would rush to work and rush back home as eagerly in the evening. I would just move through all the chores at breakneck speed, finish my dinner, and jump into bed with my crochet hook in hand. This should indicate how successful I had become in handling different 'crochet' projects. My confidence even led me to multi-task, wherein I worked on five to six projects at the same time. I could not bring myself to work on one at a time, now that I had become an experienced expert! Of course, I lessened my speed gradually after the initial elation had worn off. Quality was as important as quantity. Today, I take up just a couple of projects or even three at any given time.

NEVER GIVE UP

You must be wondering where all this is leading! You are happy that I have been bold enough to leave my home shores and venture onto alien ones. You are equally happy to know that I have not only recovered my knowledge of knitting, but also mastered a new skill, which is crochet. However, what you are really waiting for is tips on how to gain monetary rewards out of the mastery of these specific skills. After all, you have rarely heard of anyone making oodles of cash from them! Well, I may not have become a millionaire, but I have definitely managed to gain something from the publication of my talents, and hope to profit more in the future. And hope this story helps you also in making some money.

Earlier, when I was seriously engaged in perfecting my knitting, I was just content to make things for myself, or for the house. Thoughts about using my talent for initiating a business or entrepreneurship did not enter my mind at all. And that's the problem with most of us –

human beings. When we discover something great, we don't think beyond the box. We just limit our thought process and restrict our mind, maybe because of our busy lives, or maybe because we just don't want to give it a thought. This is called prejudiced thinking. So, yes, it was only after I gained confidence regarding my crocheting skills, and even began to adore crochet, that I began to give serious thought to this aspect. How glorious it would be to make some money with the help of small projects! Make money by something you love doing; make money by following your dreams. However, I would have to work out how exactly I would get these projects and how I would take them to successful completion before I actually initiated a business venture. It is all great to dream and plot about, but converting your passion into something that makes you money – requires plenty of focus, strategy, and skill perfection. And the question I had in my mind was – do I have all that?

Even now, I was more interested in inventing different types of crochet patterns, rather than creating knitting designs. Somehow, the former had become my favourite hobby, without even realising it. At the same time, I had to be honest enough to accept that I had my limitations. True, I could manage crochet reasonably well, but if I had to sell anything, it had to offer both, a display of true talent and monetary value to the purchaser. That's because doing something as a hobby and making money out of it are two different things. Therefore, for the time being, at least, I could not focus on launching my own business. I could not even think of resigning from my current place of employment. It would be best to bury such thoughts for now and focus on practice, and more practice. This did not mean that I was okay to forget about everything and remain an employee for the rest of my life. Like everyone else, I wished to be free of the employer-employee relationship, and be my own boss. I wanted the freedom, time and money to live my life the way I had always wanted to, even in an alien country. This would be possible only if I became a businessperson. Thus, I spent all my spare time on seeking a viable solution, which would enable me to continue as an employee, while at the same time, permit me to launch a business for obtaining the second income. Although doing justice to both these things was not easy, I was all ready to try it. After all, I didn't have anything to lose, so why not give it a try!

It struck me that I had to concentrate on the term, SALE, all the time, for the sake of self-motivation. I would have to find out how to make knitted or crochet items, in a way that I could sell them easily to people. Sell it to those who truly appreciated the hard work and talent going into each one of them. That's because targeting those who do not appreciate your talent or do not know the value attached to your products, will never become your potential customers. And one of the important rules in business is to target potential customers only. Nobody wants to waste their time on people who are least interested in their business.

Therefore, towards this end, I took up a research project of my own. I spent the majority of my waking hours (hours, days, and even weeks), exploring all avenues of business in the virtual world. There were so many websites displaying self-made crafts for sale. I was familiar with some of these websites but apprehensive about the genuineness of the others. Nevertheless, after pouring over the contents and web pages of several websites, I narrowed down on two of them, since they seemed perfectly authentic in nature. I even explored reviews and testimonials related to these two websites to validate their authenticity. They suggested that these two sites were perfectly genuine and trustworthy. You must have heard of them too – eBay and Etsy. If you have not, well then, let me tell you that eBay is a renowned global marketplace for buying and selling anything and everything. And Etsy offers a chance for creative mindsets to market their goods from a common platform.

I would like to give credit to these sites as they instituted an idea in my mind. Why did I not strive to create a few soft toys and sell them on these two websites? After all, people of all ages loved to have soft toys! I could even accompany the photographs of my displays with small captions and creative advertisements. Yes, this could have been done. I don't know why I didn't think about it all this while.

Having settled on this idea, I quickly got down to work. I created some marvellously cute-looking animals from crochet and advertised them on both, eBay and Etsy. I followed the steps provided on the website and publish the details needed so that users can see it all on the web. I published the ad and waited desperately for the results. You won't believe, I was so excited that I was eagerly waiting to see the response of people. I was so excited that I was refreshing the site every few minutes to see if someone sent me a message. But did I receive rich rewards immediately? Although I never it was too early to expect anything, I was keeping my fingers crossed. But unfortunately, I have to reply in the negative! It seemed as if no one was interested in even looking at them, far less in purchasing them. Obviously, only I seemed to think they were cute. Internet browsers did not feel the same about my crocheted goods. And this proved that all this wasn't that easy. You can't just publish something and expect people to buy. You really need to know how and where to advertise your business the right way. And this is exactly what the issue was – I wasn't aware of the right ways and right platforms to advertise my product.

Six months passed by, with my hopes dying each passing minute. Then, someone made me an offer on eBay, but a ridiculously low one, and just for one small soft toy. I deemed this offer as an insult to my efforts! And it's then that I lost all my hopes. Thereafter, I decided that I would never go in for crocheting again. I would not only never pick up the crochet hook ever again, but also never try to sell anything on eBay ever again! No, I would not display or try to sell anything on Etsy either! It is not worth the hard work; people do not appreciate the good work.

I said all that to myself but did I actually mean it? Wasn't my heart still set on that dream? Dream to do something of my own? Dream to make money by doing something I really liked? Despite all my bravado, it was truly hard to give up crochet, for I was so much in love with it! And with me, the thing is, if I set my heart on something, I cannot let it go that easily. Me being me, I wasn't able to let it go although I was very disappointed by the kind of response I got. Therefore, I convinced myself to continue using the crochet hook, albeit to design things that I could use for myself, or donate to friends. My friends would definitely cherish personal gifts more, in comparison to receiving store-bought ones. I believed there are still at least some people in this world who appreciate art and good work. Furthermore, the work would fill my leisure hours with fun and pleasure, for I would be engaged in a pursuit of my liking. Thus, without bothering to award too much thought to all the things that had happened during the past six months, I just continued with my crochet work. And now, I wasn't thinking about the output of all the hard work I was putting in. I was doing it just for myself – without any expectations. Trust me it felt great then. It felt great to experiment with all kinds of patterns and shapes. In fact, I could literally see myself becoming better and better at each task, as the days went by. I now truly believe that practice does make a person perfect. The finesse you get with practice is really commendable. In turn, as my talents improved, my self-esteem also began to grow, and grow! I was getting my confidence back, and I truly loved it.

Then, when I was enjoying every bit of my artwork, something splendid happened! As I became more and more involved with this unique and creative world, I discovered something amazing! I discovered "safety eyes"! If you are wondering what safety eyes are, here is a brief explanation:

What is the first thing that strikes you when you look at someone's facial features, or even an animal's face? The answer is, 'eyes', which is believed to be the most prominent feature of a person. Someone has truly said, "The eyes say it all", yes, the eyes say it all. And, the appropriate placement of safety eyes in a doll or a soft toy can make all the difference in the world to its looks. Manufacturers create safety eyes from harmless, bright plastic. They have another name in the world of toys too, which is, craft toys. Each safety eye comprises of two pieces. One of them is the straight or threaded rod, which we call the Front. The second part is the Washer. There are sufficient tutorials all over the Net, providing advice about placement, adjustment and tailoring of these safety eyes. And that's because it plays an important role in creating these toys. You must have seen in the toys shop that some of the toys look really attractive and catch your attention the moment you see them. While there are some that look ugly. If you closely observe, it is majorly the placement of these safety eyes that play the game. So, yes, coming back to the track, I learnt the trick behind placing and adjusting the safety eyes.

Once I had perused all the material related to the use of safety eyes, I was extremely keen to use them on my crocheted toys. I thought the idea was simply brilliant! Remembering that I could find anything and everything that I wanted on eBay, I browsed their online shop for these safety eyes. I found them! A pair cost £ 1.99. They seemed slightly expensive, but I desperately needed them for my soft toys. Therefore, I continued purchasing them and using them. When I sewed them onto my creations, my soft toys seemed to acquire a rare beauty! It added a different look to my toys, and I was totally elated to see. I began to work with renewed energy and hope. At the same time, I could not afford to disregard the state of my finances. Buying these items was becoming an addiction, or I should say my necessity. But, how much more could I spend on these expensive purchases, especially as I began to need more and more eyes all the time? It was time to look for sellers of safety eyes, who were willing to sell me their goods in small quantities, albeit at more affordable pricing. I was just not in the state to put in more money in my hobby, as it was just a hobby. I was not making any money out of it, as I had thought initially.

Now, if your search is genuine, you are bound to obtain genuine results! As I continued my pursuit of sellers of safety eyes, I came across an individual online, who was willing to accede to my demands. He was more than willing to offer me the pieces for a lesser price, provided I placed an order for a large quantity. Despite the affordability of the safety eyes, they would be of good quality. He wished me to purchase 1000 pieces for a price of £ 21.90 only! This was marvellous news to my ears, indeed! I couldn't control the temptation and already started dreaming about all the things I can make once I buy so many of these eyes. Believing that I may not obtain such a bargain again, I went ahead with the purchase. After the purchase, however, I began to worry about what I would do with so many eyes littering my house! Would I be able to continue to use them forever? Would my friends agree to purchase some of them? All these thoughts kept running through my mind and haunted me all the time. And I know why I was having second thoughts after I purchased them. I had invested more in this project, and although I had decided I will not think about selling them, I was just hoping some miracle happens. And that's because I needed money, and I need to do something of my own to get rid of my job. I wanted to attain financial freedom, but I was getting trapped more and more, with no results.

WAY TO SUCCESS

I couldn't control my thought processing. I kept despairing over the matter every day until the answer hit me like a lightning thunderbolt one day! There was indeed an easy way out, which had missed my attention before. However, the minute the idea popped into my head, I did not waste any more time. I just rushed to my laptop, opened it, and logged into eBay immediately. Yes, I had retained my log in details all the while. I spent some time browsing through all the categories of buy/sell, before logging out of the website. I had found the answer to the question that had been nagging me all this time. Instead of trying to sell my 'excess' goods to acquaintances and friends, I would offer them online to perfect strangers. This time, I would be the seller, and they, the buyers! Wow! Why didn't I think about it this way before? Why was I trying to sell the items only in my extended network? I would sell each pair for probably slightly lesser than the prices displayed on the site by other sellers of safety eyes. Nevertheless, I would still gain a healthy profit, because I had so many of these items with me, and I had bought them cheaply. Furthermore, I had already proved to myself that people did buy safety eyes from eBay, via my own purchases. Oh, I was wonderfully hopeful of everything falling into place and the sunshine returning to my life! But I was little apprehensive about it. Was I over expecting? Should I expect something good to happen? But I certainly didn't stop there.

Then again, I did not stop with this strategy alone. I decided to consult some experienced people who knew this domain well. That's because selling online is different from selling in physical stores. They had been in this arena for quite some time and knew how to handle everything. They willingly shared their knowledge about all the aspects of launching a small craft supplier business on the World Web, with me. These professionals gave me some handy tips too. One of them was to approach the local governmental agents. They would acquaint me with the legal aspects of initiating an online business. I was really thankful to them sharing with me all this. Anyway, I would have to approach the concerned authorities regarding documentation and registration procedures, if not now, later. Therefore, after gaining all the necessary information regarding self-employment in the virtual world, I approached them. Thankfully, the registration procedures did not take up too much time and everything went through smoothly. I also learnt that promoting what you are doing is important, in fact, it is really important. You need to spread the message and let the world know what you are trying to do. If you are not able to do that, you might be able to connect with your target audience.

Soon enough, I was able to come up with innovative advertisements regarding my business and place them at the appropriate places on the World Web. This also needs some research as you must know how and where to advertise your business if you want to succeed. Especially, in today's hi-tech society, where most of the business happens online, and even shoppers are also available online, you need to know about the right channels to showcase what you are offering. Online advertising is the key, and I understood this well. So, I learnt about some of the social media platforms that could help me spread the word and published my ads. Now, all that I had to do was to sit back and wait for the magic to begin!

Once the advertisements were ready and everything in place, I relaxed. I relaxed but I was curious to see the results. I felt like I just took a test and was waiting for the results to come. I was sure that I would not have to wait too long for something to happen. I even dreamt about all the money pouring into my coffers, as I sold my creative pieces and safety eyes in the dozens! Yes, I had already started dreaming about all the good things. Guess what happened! Nothing, yes, nothing happened! I checked the website numerous times in a day. I checked my phone too, not once, not twice, but hundreds of times. The result was the same every time – zero! Two weeks went by in a similar manner. Weren't people checking my advertisement? What was the issue? Didn't I advertise it well? Did people actually see it? Were the products so bad that no one liked it? My mind was full of thoughts and questions, and assumptions about what might have happened. But I really didn't have answers to any of my questions.

With no sale showing up at all, my worries returned with a huge bang! I was frantic! What was I to do now? I had been so positive that everything would work out and all my financial worries would be at an end. However, the situation was just becoming worse and worse. In fact, I had been right all the while, when I kept thinking and stating that the story about achieving riches through innovation, intelligence, talent, etc., was a super fairy tale and nothing more. Whoever said that freedom and talent could lead to success in life was just being fanciful! Yes, it all just sounds good and motivating but when you actually try it, you would know it is all a story making business. Nothing really works, and hard work doesn't fetch you anything. Nothing!

While I was wallowing in this ocean of self-pity and helplessness, something unexpected happened. There was a beep-beep from my mobile phone. At first, I refused to listen, feeling that it was just eBay sending me a 'watch' reminder and nothing more. However, my instincts refused to lie still, urging me to unlock the phone and check the message that had just come in. Reluctantly, I did so. I could not believe my eyes when I saw what eBay was trying to communicate to me. I cannot even explain in words what I felt upon seeing that message. EBay conveyed to me that I had just made a sale. It was my very first sale. I had sold my first pair of safety eyes! Oh, yes, miracles do happen! I could see all the negativity going away, and I was hopeful once again. Yes, good things do happen and hard work is appreciated by at least some people.

A couple of safety eyes on sale and I was ecstatic! I kept

my phone aside, pumped the air with a fisted arm a couple of times, took a deep breath and then picked up my phone again! This was such a tiny start to all the dreams that I had, but I was happy to get a start nonetheless. Yes, this was one ray of hope. Just one sale was enough to make me happy. I was happy that it at least started. Gathering all my happiness, I made sure I packed and shipped the product carefully to the customer, and hoped that he leaves me a good review on my new site to boost further sales. I had also learnt that sales and good reviews are two very crucial elements of any business. You should work on driving more sales and getting good reviews. Reviews are important because these days people check the product reviews before making their purchase decisions, and hence they play an important role in your success. So, I wanted more sales to happen and more reviews – positive ones, of course as these two are the key elements of any growing business. And I wanted to have a business of my own.

Now that I had made my first sale, I naturally expected rest to trickle in like water from a fountain. And that's very natural – we, human beings are greedy. When something positive happens, our expectations increase and we want it to happen again – over and over again. These expectations become problematic when they turn into over expectations. And then, I was back to staring at my phone for hundreds of minutes each day, waiting for it to beep with the confirmation of my next sale. I thought I was going to be on a roll, but alas! That didn't happen! I finally accepted that that one sale was a fluke; something that happened on the whim of one of the buyers who happened to stumble upon my website, and that was that.

Rather than letting the absence of sales pull me down, I decided to re-focus on making my crochet toys better and seeking ideas on how else I could monetise my site. Of course, I cannot just sit and wait for the sales to happen. It doesn't work that way, and I had to continue focusing on other things also. And when I was dealing with all this, my boyfriend was a great support to me. He told me to never give up and always look forward to what could happen. I was so thankful to have such an understanding and supportive partner throughout my ups and downs! At times, all you need is mental support and little motivation – someone who can tell you that things will fall into place; someone to hold you when you feel low. Thankfully, I had him by my side. He was always there for me, no matter what.

So I did what I do best. I shrugged off my doubts, kept my optimism high, and continued with doing what I love. It was this realisation that I loved soft toys and crocheting them that led me to a whole new chapter in my struggling career path! I am glad that I took several steps and measures to get to where I am now. I am glad my love for this cure little thing never faded, and I continued doing what I was good at. The baby steps I took towards my financial and personal independence gave me the strength to wither all the storms, big and small, that came my way. I could see myself failing so many times, but each time I got up and started again. I am so happy and proud of myself when I think of all the times that I could have ducked out of the race but I never did. After all, I had blown the whistle, struggled to overcome chest-high hurdles, and race towards the finishing line that I had set. I was my own biggest competitor. So when I beat off my dispiritedness and lethargy, I was evolving myself into a better me! And this is the best way to learn something. When you get something the hard way, you know the value of that thing, and you cherish it always. Yes, I am seeing the brighter side of it – the side that led me to the right path to success.

Emotions and dreams aside, I thought to myself – it's time I get business-wise. It was all well and good to indulge myself in making fancy toys and watching kids' faces light up, but I had my ambition to feed too. Having a hobby is good but money is really important. I was still hungry for making it big by my own rights, and continue to have a viable business that would do well enough for me to give the corporate world a complete pass. So while I continued making toys, I kept racking my brain to find a way to get my business up and running.

A couple of days later, I got another beep from my now-long-forgotten phone. I really wanted it from my so-called favourite site again. And yes, I was right this time. It seemed like someone was on a crocheting spree and need a dozen pairs of safety eyes! That was a whopper of a sale for me, obviously, and I was elated that a few more of the products I'd put up for sale were garnering attention. And this time, it couldn't be a fluke. So, yes, people were buying my products, and it was working. Also, I was happy to know that there are others also in this world who are making cute little toys using these safety eyes. That's why whenever there was a sale, my boyfriend and I used to look at each other and smile as this sale was an indication that the buyer is making a cute little teddy, just the way I do, for happiness and pleasure.

To my surprise, the week that I made a sale of those dozen safety eyes, I made a few more sales. It wasn't a number to write home about, but in my eyes, the safety eyes getting cleared out meant my website was getting the attention it should. And that's a big thing in itself. In this world where there is neck-to-neck competition for everything, if people are checking out your website, it is really worth the happiness. This means the awareness is there and people are noticing your work. This was a motivation and I was elated. My spirits came up slowly, and I vowed to double my efforts to make this business thrive in one way or the other. I knew I had the potential to crochet and make interesting items. The game had just started and I had to put in place lot of strategies and plans to make it big. This was just the trailer; I wanted the entire movie to get several likes – 'Likes', yes, that's what gets counted in today's digital world. Although I didn't know much about marketing and advertising, especially in this e-world, I know that these so-called 'Likes and shares' have captured the market. Your success is measured in terms of these likes, comments and shares. But for now, what remained to be seen was my determination that made me as successful in the field of business too.

And then I could see it happening; I could see things changing for good. After the first sale, things started falling into place and I was selling at least two eyes every day. This was a great number. There were, of course days when I didn't sell any, but then there were also days when I would sell 4 or 5, or even more. Then there were days when I found myself to be doing a sale of 14 items in a week. And let me tell you that I was really proud of myself. From nothing to 14 – that was really awesome. But somewhere deep inside, I kept thinking if that was all I wanted. Was that enough to make me happy? Was that my dream? Should I continue doing how I was doing? I didn't know if that was "ALL" I wanted in life to attain my financial freedom, and then eventually I realized that I need more. I realized that I need more from life and therefore I put in more effort, more hard work and more time. I didn't stop there; I continued. And to my surprise, after a year of hard work and patience, I could build my own company – a company with 1402 products. Yes, I had my own company, my own logo, my own brand, and I was doing a sale of approximately 48 items per day, and this number was constantly growing. Yes, the number was growing each day! And I understood that it's all about time and hard work. The more time and effort I was putting, the more output I was getting. With time, I could see my business thriving! From zero to 48 to WOW! But, was it real? Or was it just a dream? I was confused but no, it was actually happening. It was real and my dream was transforming into reality. I could see it happen.

And then another great thing happened. While I was busy with building my brand, my business, and multiply the numbers, I got a call from Royal Mail (Royal Mail is UK's most trusted company for parcels and letters delivery). But why would Royal Main call me? Can you guess what they told me? Well, they told me something that I couldn't believe and it took me a couple of minutes to realize what I heard was true. I could believe my ears when I heard that. Royal Mail offered me a business contract as they found out high activity from my account. Yes, I was using their service extensively and that's because I was buying more and more labels. So, yes, they wanted to offer me a contract. Really!!! It was indeed a really big thing for me. But it was happening, in reality.

THE MOTIVATION FOR EVERYONE

So, this is my story – my story that tells you how I fell and then stood up. You can see how I chased my dream, by taking baby steps. I failed and failed, at every step but I did get back. I stood up leaving all the failures behind as I didn't lose my focus. I knew exactly what I wanted – I wanted to attain financial freedom by doing something I loved. And I proved myself that hard work and patience pays back; it doesn't go in vain. It is just the matter of time, and if you are really dedicated, you will get what you want in life. And this is true, you can see it for yourself. Today, I have my own company and people know me for my work. I have made my identity in this world. People appreciate my work.

So, I want to tell you that chasing your dreams is not wasting time; it pays back. And trust me if I can do it, each one of you can transform your dream into reality. Yes, you can do it. All you need is self-realization. You should know what you want, and once you are clear about your goals, there is no stopping, no looking back. If you do not take the initiative and remain stuck with your 9-5 "secured" job, you will never attain financial freedom. And one day, you will realize that secured job was actually not secure. You were just tied in a trap. So, the sooner you realize, the sooner you will be able to transform your dreams into reality. But if you are too scared of taking risks, I am sorry but you will be trapped for rest of your life.

Failure will come, and there will be many obstacles in your way. Of course, attaining financial freedom isn't easy; it is a path full of horns. You should know how to overcome and come out with flying colours. The day you know this, you will move only in upward direction. So, yes, it's for everyone – each one of us. Don't look back. Just stay focused and stay committed, and you will get it!

ABOUT THE AUTHOR

Dora Gomory is a small-town girl, who grew up with a dream of becoming rich and living a quality life. She always wanted to attain financial freedom, but not by doing what everyone else is doing. She wanted to do something different, something that could give your happiness. She was never interested in a regular 9-5 job, as she wanted to attain financial freedom by doing something she loved to. With a 'never give up, never lose hopes' attitude, she started knitting and crocheting, and turned this hobby into something big – big enough to earn her living, and chasing her dreams. Through this book, she has shared her journey of how she started all this and how she turned it into something really amazing; what difficulties she faced by still managed to make it happen. When you really love your job, no one can stop you from growing as you give your heart and soul to it. She has beautifully depicted how her hard work and patience helped her in each and every step.

www.ingramcontent.com/pod-product-compliance
Lightning Source LLC
Chambersburg PA
CBHW030057230526
45471CB00003B/1131